T0381127

For THE SAKE *of* SHARING

A Little Poetry and

Random Threads

of Transformative Thinking

QUINTANA

BALBOA.PRESS
A DIVISION OF HAY HOUSE

Balboa Press books may be ordered through booksellers or by contacting:

Balboa Press
A Division of Hay House
1663 Liberty Drive
Bloomington, IN 47403
www.balboapress.com
844-682-1282

Because of the dynamic nature of the Internet, any web addresses or links contained in this book may have changed since publication and may no longer be valid. The views expressed in this work are solely those of the author and do not necessarily reflect the views of the publisher, and the publisher hereby disclaims any responsibility for them.

The author of this book does not dispense medical advice or prescribe the use of any technique as a form of treatment for physical, emotional, or medical problems without the advice of a physician, either directly or indirectly. The intent of the author is only to offer information of a general nature to help you in your quest for emotional and spiritual well-being. In the event you use any of the information in this book for yourself, which is your constitutional right, the author and the publisher assume no responsibility for your actions.

Scripture quotations marked KJV are from the Holy Bible, King James Version (Authorized Version). First published in 1611. Quoted from the KJV Classic Reference Bible, Copyright © 1983 by The Zondervan Corporation.

Cover art by Quintana
Illustrations and photographs by Quintana

Print information available on the last page.

ISBN: 979-8-7652-4884-3 (sc)
ISBN: 979-8-7652-4886-7 (hc)
ISBN: 979-8-7652-4885-0 (e)

Library of Congress Control Number: 2024900539

Balboa Press rev. date: 03/05/2024

To Michelle, my sister and best friend, who supports me in all my creative endeavors, patiently listens to my flights of fancy, and lovingly chides me with logic when my thinking becomes nebulous. I love you.

The substance of things hoped for and the evidence of things not seen.

Hebrews 11:1 (KJV)

Upward movement;
You can begin just where you are.
Fill your heart with love and praise
and gratitude.

The secret you will discover is that upward
movement truly begins from within.

CONTENTS

CONTENTS

POEMS

ILLUSTRATIONS

ACKNOWLEDGMENTS

I choose to acknowledge God. Now in the winter season of my life, I can look back and recognize that He has provided everything I have ever needed in my life, whether it was a hard lesson intended to reign me in or wake me up, or a little miracle to remind me of who I am. Never negligent but ever vigilant; a loving Father devoted to guiding my steps, constantly revealing the love that is His grace, even during times when I couldn't see the big picture and times when surrender brought peace.

DOVE

INTRODUCTION

Grace

We only ever work to emulate Him,
That which is a part of us, unaware.
Aware is most like Him.

That poem is merely a reverent declaration and a fervent prayer. Hope lies in our deepest desire to evolve, to do good, to do no harm, and to experience that seemingly elusive evolution of the soul—the great awakening spoken of by scholars, monks, and devotees alike. Take note that the last line is really a twofold statement, both a declaration and a question, as we could never be just like Him because not one of us is perfect, no matter how much we desire or aspire to be.

We all fall short of perfection. Awareness is just the first step on a particular path. Not all paths lead in the same direction, which is to say, we all have the inalienable right of choice and free will.

Seeking to have a personal relationship with God, the knowledge and heartfelt faith that Christ is the absolute truth, the epitome of *love* in one's life, and your innermost confidant and constant companion must always be the goal.

How many ways can we express that knowledge mindfully or consciously? Yet we find the idea fleeting and disappointing as our other relationships collide or combust and we fall short of our own aspirations. Our desire is to live the fairy tale, and some of us seem always to look in the wrong places.

Considering this, then the concept of identity, of being the archetypal friend or lover, is a precarious undertaking. These are the people, our friends and lovers, we invariably look to as our knights in shining armor. When they fall off that horse, we are bankrupt, broken, and in denial of the fact that the entire event was a collaborative venture.

You get the idea. Life is just a fairy tale, or is it? This is what we've been taught and, some would say, programmed to believe since childhood. Someone is eventually coming to save us or take care of us. Someone will save us from our suffering and desperation, and that someone will fulfill all our needs and protect us from harm, have our backs, and give us the solutions to all of our problems.

The real hope might be that we want to be saved from ourselves. The need to belong, and, yes, even the need to be known, recognized, respected as an equal, and desired is innate in our DNA. Thank God, and so we seek. It's all part of our blueprint.

Believe that no matter how minute the truth of that aspect of your personality is evident to you, you can trust that God knows who you are. He knows you in the deepest recesses of your soul, as do you.

I'm sure that fear is what keeps us from owning our truth. F.E.A.R.—false expectations appearing real. You know what I'm talking about; I'm afraid of what might happen, no matter how unlikely the scenario I conjure up in my mind.

I can't tell you which is more alarming, that you know who you are or that God knows who you are. This is a good reason to contemplate the meaning of the words reverence and respect. Reverence and respect for God, for yourself, and then for everyone else.

Even then, in your heart, the hope somehow, sometimes seems unrequited. If you think about it logically, we do fall short of the mark. We may not be perfect, but we are all human.

You knowing who you are is really no big deal;

you can hide that from almost everyone, including yourself, but you cannot hide who you are from God.

Realizing that you just might ultimately be responsible for your life, your soul, means to me that the only truth you will ever find is within yourself. Whether you believe in a higher source, the universe, or nothing, this is ultimately your choice.

I choose to believe in God. Within myself is where I find God. I declare; *I am*. I am you, you are me, and here we all are, just being human differently.

I *am* until we aren't. We disagree on politics, religion, lifestyle, origin, DNA, class, and tribe. It's confusing, frustrating, fascinating, and beautiful.

No matter what we choose to believe in, what state of consciousness we find ourselves in, or what country we reside in, whether you choose to believe in God or not, we are all in this together. No one is going to get out of here unscathed.

I offer you some spontaneous threads of thought, a little poetry, and a bit of art, along with a few illuminating quotes from others who've touched my soul. It's all very much a part of my own search for adventure. Simply put, I'm one of many expressing my feelings with words to create a painting that you might find touches something in you, and as the title portends, this is, after all, just for the sake of sharing.

POETRY

POETRY

Life

I want to run, I want to hide, I'm frightened; don't you see?
I'm scared of life and scared of love
but mostly scared of me.
Just when I think I know it all, I find this cannot be.
'Tis then I close my eyes in fright and all caves in on me.
"Are you a man, or are you mouse?"
I think the phrase does go,
But, Lord, I'm neither man nor mouse,
just woman. Don't you know?
At times I want the hearth and home,
but then again, I find
That love doth make a prisoner, imprisoned by the mind.
To free my mind and stand alone is
total satisfaction, then love
Comes knocking on my door, and love is life's attraction.
So once again the futile question
clouds my eyes from seeing
That truth is just and love's a must, but life is in the being.

As a very little girl sitting on the front porch stoop, I was contemplating an epiphany that most of the adults around me, who were in charge of my life, were totally clueless about themselves. I remember thinking that this was all just going to be an adventure. I was sure I would survive because somehow, deep down from somewhere within me, I just knew the truth: that there was no such thing as death. This realization has stuck with me all my life.

Why?

Why is it life doth emulate
Itself among the flowers?
Once seed, once bud,
And true to fate,
In full bloom, ends its hours.

What of Death?

How oft' I've wondered and I've said,
"Why do the flowers die?"
But then, said death, "Oh do not fear, for just a myth am I."
The flowers simply go to sleep, and then again in spring
It's from the ground they start to
peak and all their colors sing.
The summer finds them blooming
full, their glory, splendor vast.
Then fall begins to let them know the day is almost past.
Soon winter comes and once again
the cold will bring them in.
And sleep will come to keep them safe
till spring begins to grin.
There is no death. I tell you true: eternity is real.
And, like the flowers, earth and you
will live through my ordeal.
There is no death. I tell you this. But
slumbers peaceful best.
And death is nothing save a myth;
God keeps you while you rest.

He who fears death fears either unconsciousness or another sort of consciousness. Now if you will no longer be conscious, you will not be conscious either of anything bad. If you are to take on a different consciousness, you will be a different being and life will not cease. (Marcus Aurelius)

Did you stop to wonder what the physical body was for, why I imprisoned your soul within one? Did the tomato seed stop to wonder why its life force was imprisoned in the molecules of the seed? Did it look forward to the time when the seed would die of old age and set its life force free? No, it realized instead that it was in the seed for a purpose, that through the seed it could work its way to full maturity, to full fruition. It realized that within the seed its divine pattern was contained. (Ruby Nelson)

It seems to me that we set ourselves up, and the joke is on us as we could never live up to what we personally perceive as perfection. We might well be legends in our own minds, but truly it's our secret personal expectations of ourselves and our fears of living up to the expectations of others around us that can plague us with doubt. As human beings we are all codependent. It's part of the human condition.

This is not a big secret. Actually, it could be an

unrealized gift. We've simply failed to completely understand the truth of codependency or what it looks like to implement it in a loving, positive way. We need each other, and that's a fact.

We have to laugh at each other as we seem to lack the ability to be more than self-absorbed at any given moment. Especially in this era, this day and age. In a time when we should respect one another, trust in faith, and love our ever-changing expression of diversity, we are way too opinionated and way too self-righteous. I ask you, Is our self-righteousness aimed in the wrong direction? How right do you feel you have to be, and where do you see respect in all the commotion?

We still fall way short concerning forgiveness. For surely we are less forgiving of each other than God or Jesus Christ or the Holy Spirit, for that matter. I hope that I will eventually belong to a complete understanding of who I am, and in the end, this is the truth I must come face to face with. This is the truth I must honor in my own soul because I know who I am.

I, of myself, really know nothing as factual, for at best, the mind has only impressions and presumptions. Life "makes sense" solely in retrospect. (David Hawkins)

Some of us believe that everything happens in our lives for a reason, and I happen to be one of those people. There is the good, the bad, and the ugly, and then there are the miracles. Everyone has a story that needs to be shared, should be shared, and in that sharing we find our own humanity. Reading someone else's story allows us to see parts of ourselves. It allows us to recognize our own feelings and to know that we are not alone.

It takes courage to tell the whole truth and nothing but the truth. This is how I see it; sometimes telling your story is the only way to face your fears, and sometimes when you face your biggest fears you begin to realize that this is the only way to find your miracles. Your story might be my miracle, and my story might be your saving grace. It's the sharing that's important.

October

I'm not sure that I know what I think that I know.
I'm not sure that my feelings are real,
But sometimes I'm sure that I'm crazy to think
I should care what I think or I feel.

S.E.L.F.—spiritual, emotional life force

L. O. V. E.—life objectified; victory everlasting

LOVE

All the Children

All the children have slept and must now be awakened,
For together as children, we are not forsaken.
Our God, in His mercy, has made us as one,
And together, with love, His task will be done.

As children, we know that our Father is just,
And His love is our truth, and in Him we must trust.
It is He who doth breathe every breath that we take;
It is peace that He wishes all children to make.

ALL THE CHILDREN

Life is our biggest mystery. Who are we, where do we come from, how long have we been here, and how long do we have? But the most important question I find for everyone is, What is our purpose?

Questions and Answers

When I try to write and make it rhyme, it's difficult at best.
Then when I least expect a rhyme,
it flows from where I rest.
I used to hide and felt each rhyme
and message was for me,
But love and sharing, peace and light,
are also meant for thee.
One lesson learned and understood,
I'm grateful for the task.
Remember: when you need to know, the thing to do is ask.
I can't say why the answers come for me in rhythmic time.
With honesty and harmony, I know the words aren't mine.
Just remember: ask your questions,
let them go, and do not fear,
But trust, no matter how they come, an answer will apear.

Sanity

I'm writing things that speak in rhyme
and lessons are the theme,
But somehow, I've begun to see the lessons there for me.
In writing from a question asked, an answer does appear,
As though the words were from the
past, returning to my ears.
I find that I'm compelled to write and
make some final statement,
'Tis then I find that sanity becomes a rude fixation.

SANITY

From Within

It is I, it is you, and again, as before, the
lyrics I sing are poetic and more.
The answers you seek to the questions you've asked are
contained in my words, in the book from the past.
There are men, who are like me, and
like me, they are more,
But, as I was I am—only I am the door.
It was God who did send me, and to God I returned,
And the great emulations are merely sojourned.
'Twas our Father who sent me, and
again I will be, as I am,
But you cannot be me.

Seeking

O God, our God, where do You live,
atop a hill or mountain?
Give me truth and give me love, for
I've been searching far above
When I should be looking deep inside
and showing all the others;
Ride with me and take me home, for
You, O God, I should have known
Are always very close at hand with
love for me and no demands.
Save one, the one I do not show I
understand, and yet I know
I am and I will always be with You, O Lord, for eternity.

An Answer to a Prayer

It's God, you know, who speaks to you;
it's God who lives within,
And once you understand this truth, eternal life begins.
But this is just the start, you know;
there's more that you must learn.
If God exists beneath the skin, it's
God from whom you turn,
When you search and seek, still
looking for your own identity,
So search no more, have peace of mind.
With God, it's God you be.
One tiny part of one big whole, an
atom of the mass; you are
The thing you're looking for. Your search must end, at last.

A Riddle

How can one be and yet not be,
Together and apart, a particle of eternity?
That which is many, yet together is one.
The answer is here: in the end, you've begun.

PARTICLES

Untitled

It is I who am in you, and I who am near.

It is I who did give you all you have here.

It is time that distracts you and love you've been seeking.

When will you learn that you are what you seek?

Look deep within you to find where I live;

I've always been with you and willing to give.

When you discover the "I" in the "you,"

Then you will know, you are me, I *am* you.

I Am

I *am*, you are,

We are together.

I *am*, you are, we will not die.

I *am*, you are, we are forever.

I *am* what you are.

I *am* is the tie.

Another Message

When you finally learn just who you are,
Who God is,
Then you'll know
The lessons you were sent to learn,
Then teach before you go.

The meaning in life is to find your gift, The
purpose of life is to give it away. (Pablo Picasso)

Faith and Trust

The flesh is not the thing to trust,
For wise men always know
That passion comes from deep within
But fashions come and go.
It's trust and faith that stand alone
When fear and strife are found.
It's trust that keeps your heart so near
And faith that keeps us bound.
I will not speak of circumstance;
I know not what you seek.
I only know that faith and trust
Are things I need to keep.
When all else fails and love grows weak,
And pride has given in,
It's trust and faith that hold me up
And strengthen me within.

End the delusion of time. Nothing exists outside the now. (Eckhart Tolle)

The past gives you an identity and the future holds the promise of salvation. Both are illusions. (Eckhart Tolle)

Life is lived in the extra beats we hold as time unfolds. Soon, the two beats become four, four become eight, and eventually we will have mastered the art of experiencing life, of feeling who we are and where we are on our path to greatness, of creating real moments, of living as joyous masters in the infinate and divine Freedom of Now. (Brendon Burchard)

NOW

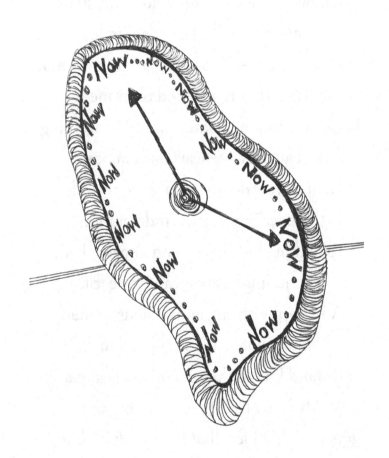

Now

I know where I am, and I do understand
That *now* is the best place to be.
But sometimes, it seems, my heart and my mind,
Have different agendas for me.
Logically thinking, I know what I'm drinking,
And joy fills my heart on command,
Then sorrow decides, that joy only hides,
The feelings I don't understand,
I shouldn't know hate, and anger is bad,
But feelings were meant to be felt.
And happy or sad, even jealous or mad,
I know *now* is where they all melt.
My mind knows that *now* is a logical place,
My heart feels that *now* I am safe.
It is *now* that I feel that I know what I know,
And it's *now* that I *am* in God's grace.

At Thirty-Two

I say to you, the things I knew, when I knew everything,
Were lost through time but never left,
For love's that very thing.
I do not speak of love for man,
though that is partially true,
I speak of love as peace of mind,
In God's own point of view.

GRACE AND GRATITUDE

Remember, just a little pure awareness relieves a soul of great fear. (Bhagavad Gita)

Awareness of a thought—at its' conception—takes place in a confident and quiet mind—completely at ease with its' role as witness to creation. (Dr. Frank Kinslow)

Veils

It's true, you see, the things we said.
We told you what would be.
It's true, we know, you listened well,
And now the truth is free.
Keep on this path, and keep aware;
Keep light about your head.
There's nothing more that need be done,
As this was also said.
The bonds you feared are almost gone,
And love will now prevail, for love has lit the darkness,
And it's time to lift the veils.

Love, Peace, and Truth

From love and peace the truth will come,
And truth is all that matters.
For you will see that practicalities are thoughts
That soon get scattered.
If all the world would join together, unite in love and peace,
Then all the world would soon discover
That strife and pain would cease.
For each man comes and each man goes,
From love and back again,
To know and learn the needed lessons,
From the beginning until the end.

Directions

I choose life and love and gratitude
And health and wealth and attitude.
Forever is the latitude
As time becomes a platitude,
But God, O God,
He is our longitude.

I Am What I Am

I am what I am, and nothing more,
And all that I am, I have been before.
Though before, I have been what I was, as I am.
I still havent been the best that I can.

ME, MYSELF, AND I

Love

Love is all we need to share, and love is much denied,
But should we just begin to care, 'tis love we can not hide.

Self-Aware

We talk of peace and speak of love, yet in our haste,
The thoughts get shoved around the
truth instead of through,
To make aware the 1 of you.
Our meditations must be done, and we
must work for truth to come
That we might live and walk the same,
To show our brothers
The peace attained.

A Simple Rhyme

I write in rhyme for you to read, a song that lets you listen.
My voice in time will show the need
for you to learn this lesson:
That you and I are once again together,
as before, united and beginning
Once again, again once more.

When this particular poem came to me, I thought that it spoke about reincarnation, as I was investigating such a train of thought at the time. Comparative religions is a healthy subject of inquiry. What's interesting is how you can read something, derive a specific meaning, and then later, maybe even years later, read the same words and understand them in a completely different way. Although at one time I did entertain the idea of reincarnation, I understand this poem now as having more to do with forgiveness, both the idea of God's forgiveness toward us as well as our forgiveness of each other.

That being said, while I no longer ascribe to

Buddha's premise regarding reincarnation, nor can I agree with the Hinduism version, I continue to seek to understand eternity in relation to the possibility of reincarnation.

Now I know that word does not appear anywhere in the Bible, so this is nothing more than a quest to understand. After all, I'm just sharing.

First, let me say that I believe all religions have purpose and are beautiful in that they present a pathway to pursue personal truth. I believe we're all on one path or another, pursuing our own understanding of truth—the purpose for our existence, the meaning of life. I also know that in the end, we all end up in the same place. We long to know the answers to the questions; Is this all there is? Is there something more? Is there life after death? Is eternity real?

Reincarnation and resurrection. What is the difference? In a conversation with Nicodemus Jesus said, "Verily, verily, I say unto thee, Except a man be born again, he cannot see the kingdom of God" (John 3:3 KJV). Those words have prompted several branches of Christianity to adopt the moniker born-again. Supposing- that we have faith in Jesus, whose mission was to show us the way, that He was speaking of resurrection and not reincarnation, we too might follow to experience eternity with God.

We will all experience death. Is death final? Most of us believe in the soul, that we have one. Something that is a part of us but bigger than ourselves. What does it mean when we speak about our higher selves?

This is just a train of thought, so to speak, but I am positive that we are more than our physical bodies, we do have a soul, and we can, indeed, communicate with our higher selves. What if reincarnation is a reality that happens just once, meaning we might experience a resurrection when we die? Our bodies will die and we will be born again. Ashes to ashes, dust to dust. Born of spirit.

The butterfly exists within the caterpillar, which symbolically, as it creates its cocoon, effectually dies, never to be a caterpillar again but a magnificently beautiful winged creature. The DNA of the caterpillar includes the butterfly as the caterpillar houses the seed that, in full bloom, reveals the butterfly.

Logically, the higher being exists within the caterpillar. The caterpillar is born again to live a different life, no longer crawling on the ground but taking flight. Is the caterpillar reincarnated or resurrected? Is reincarnation possibly explained by way of resurrection? I leave you for a while to contemplate these questions.

Reincarnation versus resurrection. I know they are very different.

> What Jesus did for us on the cross is greater than anything anyone has done to us. (Pastor Melissa Scott)

Purpose

I try to write a simple thought, and
soon I find that it is not,
And words I started out to use mean
something different, something new.
If you can read the words behind the
words you read from me,
Then listen well, and I will tell the message rhythmically.
It's someone else's words you read; it's
me who writes them down,
And though they seem of poetry, a lesson might be found.
If I were you and you were me, you'd
understand the riddle,
For all who read and understand
are standing in the middle.
Which way is up, which way is down?
The road is straight and narrow.
Make up your mind, take time for thyne,
for thyne and mine tomorrow.

Time

It's time that ties you, peace that binds
you, love that keeps you near.
From one to all, I say this now, and all should try to hear:
Give love, give peace to all you meet before time disappears.

The Messenger

A winged angel came to say that life and love's the only way
To show our Lord you understand that
it is He that doth command.
A winged angel said to me, "It's time to go and look and see
What happens when we give up fairy tales,
And time itself is such a fairy tale."

Pretending

Pretend you are an animal; pretend that you can fly.
Pretend can become a game when you guess at life's reply.

Feelings

Who was it that said that pain is
good and desperation's kin?
A poet or a painter, he whose heart was sealed within,
Who understands that pain doth bring
the words that cannot come
And desperation's song will sing a painting when it's done.
He understands the silence of the souls that cannot speak;
He feels the desperation of a poet's pen and ink.
He must have touched His canvas
with a brush of hue to learn
The peace that comes from statements made
when words cannot be turned.

Repeating Lessons

If life did offer one short dance,
And you give up your only chance,
What would you give to make ammends,
When all your life seems but pretence.
How do you think of God's great love,
Your life, a gift, to push or shove?
Just wait, the truth becomes so clear,
For in the end, you'll shed a tear.

Don't you find it maddening to think that you understand and have dealt with a specific lesson only to be confronted with that very same lesson again? You believe that you have put the situation to rest so you can move on in life, find gratitude in the growth, but you can't. What was it that you missed? What part haven't you scrutinized? How much more of the onion needs to be peeled?

Meditation

I wonder, ponder, and meditate on all the things
that people hate, and life seems nothing more
than this, for love is missing, far from bliss.
Why do we have such hateful hearts, and
what becomes of all false starts?
A lesson from within comes through to
teach that I'm the same as you.
And while the learning takes such time, and while
the yearning seems sublime, I wait and wonder
all the day, *oh when will God begin to play?*
Or has He been a constant player, unseen
love from life's own prayer?
Give praise for yet another day when love will
come with hope to stay, to give you yet another
chance to learn to sing and learn to dance.

THE DANCE

January

It's time again to let you know that I am still within.

For all who seek the light and peace, I wish to now begin,

To let you know I'm glad for you and

tell you that I'm proud,

For you are taking giant steps, our voice is sounding loud.

Our peaceful song is being heard,

our love is spreading fast,

And soon for all, truth will be learned,

'tis fear will be outcast.

May

I am a loner, yet not alone; I am skin, and I am bones.

I'm asking for a revelation and expect I will be shown

Why within I know I'm living but this shell is not my home.

Why do I feel so fractured; can you help me to discern

Why one part seems aware of light,

the other seems infirm?

My purpose brings me truth and love; joy teaches me I can,

I love the light and understand that part that is *I am*.

The other part, I guess I know, is vital to your scheme.

Salvation is the gift of life, to learn I am redeemed.

OUR FIRST TEACHERS

Our very first teachers in life are our parents. We learn how to trust, stand, walk, and run from them. Hopefully we learn something about love and acceptance too. Basically, we learn how to be in the world. Good, bad, or indifferent, these are our first teachers who bear a great responsibility, and they set our feet on our path in life. Good, bad, or indifferent, the reason we need to honor our mother and father is that they were the vehicle by which we came into this world. The lessons we learn going forward are part of our own blueprint; our purpose in life is to honor that contract.

Next, we enter school. We learn how to be social beings. This is a whole new set of lessons that cause us to begin to adjust our understandings of who we are. From our teachers to our peers, our very foundation determines how we relate and grow from this point forward. We never stop adjusting our self-image and our belief systems based on what we've learned from our first teachers and then from our life experiences. Life seems to be a constant quest to understand who we are, why we are, and what it all means.

If we're lucky, we learn how to pick ourselves up after we fall, and if we're smart, we learn something new from each experience.

Some of us eventually learn that if we keep beating our heads against the wall, it might be time to stop and go in another direction. Eventually we move on. Life is good. We pack our bags with all the lessons we've gained until the bags begin to get so heavy that we realize it's time to sort through everything, throw out what no longer serves us, and take stock in those things we deem important to keep.

> We can not teach people anything: We can only help them discover it in themselves. (Galileo)

One of my favorite books is *The Motivation Manifesto: 9 Declarations to Claim Your Personal Power* by Brendon Burchard. In the fourth declaration, "We Shall Advance With Abandon," he says, "You are responsible for your reality. Decide what you want of the world and go make it happen. No clarity, no change, no goals, no growth."

FIRST TEACHERS

KNOWING IS GROWING

Once you know something, you can't unknow it in your heart; you will know a thing to be truth or not. Once you hear something, you can't unhear it. It will ring in your heart forever. Once you see something, you can't unsee it in your mind. It will be burned into your mind forever so that you, once you have opened your heart, will hear and see things that you will know as truth. You will recognize them because you will know them in your heart forever.

You can try to ignore it, to deny it, even to yourself, but once you know a thing as truth, you cannot unknow it; you can only grow in your knowledge.

So then everything you see and hear and know in your heart as truth will follow you all the days of your life. Some of those things will never change but some will evolve. You will grow to have a new perception of those same concepts. Truth is like a seed planted in your heart—it will still be there as a fundamental truth for you but the knowledge of it will evolve and grow into a new understanding. We call this an epiphany. The words haven't changed, but you perceive them in a new light. Like a child who has no understanding of the concept of time, you grow into your knowledge just as a child learns the meaning of and the difference between hours, days, months and years. God is such a truth for me, as is love, grace, forgiveness, and peace. I am grateful for the opportunity to evolve in my understanding of these things everyday.

STREAMING THOUGHT

Christ said, "I am the way, and the truth and the life. No one comes to the Father except through me" (John 14:6 KJV). I do believe Jesus was the way-shower, if you will.

> He that hath seen me hath seen the Father.
> (John 14:9 KJV)

If you say, "I am God," know that it's true that He created us in His image so we are part of but never equal to God. We all possess the gift of creativity. You could ask yourself if God created man or if man created God. I believe I know the answer.

Even Jesus submitted to the will of the Father, God. He performed no miracles or healings outside of God's will. He wasn't less than God but part of God; He was the Son of God and man, a gift from God to His children to help them understand the deep abiding love of the Father for His children, His creation.

Jesus said that you cannot enter the kingdom of

God (see God) but by Him (Jesus) who followed the will of the Father, God.

God is always first and foremost the Almighty. Jesus, the Son of God, is part of the Godhead, as is the Holy Spirit. We understand this as the trinity. All aspects of God—Father, Son, and Holy Spirit—are one and the same.

I believe I can say, "I am God" because I am made in His image but not equal to God. God is my Father, and Jesus Christ is my Savior, sent by God to show me the way (the truth), and the Holy Spirit is God's grace that dwells within me.

> I have said, Ye are all gods; And all of you are children of the most High. (Psalm 82:6 KJV)

I've heard this scripture expressed differently in movies as ye are Gods and you know it not, or something similar, alluding to the idea that we are actually Gods. Many self-help books hint at this idea when they say, *I am God*. Does this mean we are equal to God or belonging to God? One of these ideas seems to be egotistical and narcissistic. One of these statements seem to lack both humility and gratitude.

I can say with confidence, "I am God," but I think it's a tricky statement. I hear it as a declaration, an understanding that I am of God, from God, and He is my Father, my Maker. I did not create myself or my soul. I exist because of Him. I am not equal to Him. His Grace resides within me.

We have free will, which means we are free to discern what we believe and to have faith in what we believe. Faith is an action based on belief and sustained by confidence.

I am the way, the truth and the light. He was born; He came to dwell among us and teach us, and He told us what would happen. He died, paid with His earthly incarnation, or His life, for our sins, past, present, and future. He was resurrected. That is the light at the end of the tunnel. If the resurrection did not happen, then we believe in vain.

We are all sinners. This is just a fact. I think this is what is meant by original sin, which speaks to our inheritance (Adam and Eve in the garden). It's in our DNA. Even though a newborn babe is innocent, the seed exists within. I'm thinking of the parable of the sower. The seed is planted. Will it be wheat or tares? You grow up in the field, which is the world; you have free will, freedom of choice. The true purpose in life is to make that ultimate choice. Do you believe in God? Do you have faith in Jesus? Does eternity exist as your reality?

The purpose of Jesus walking among us was very simple: to show that we are all going to experience a death at some point on our path here on earth (born again). We can choose to have faith in Jesus, as He showed us the way. We can choose to believe in the resurrection of Christ as the light, which is the promise from God of a new beginning and the promise to heal the mistake made in the garden (forgiveness for the past). Once you know a thing as truth, you know it forever.

You can choose not to believe. That's it; a simple either-or scenario. It is completely your choice, which is the purpose of the gift of free will.

The good news is what is asked of us: to love God with all our heart and all our soul and to treat our neighbor as ourself. We are to have love and respect and forgiveness for each other. Do you love and respect and forgive yourself?

We are to believe, yes, but also have faith. Jesus shed His blood on the cross, He died to pay for our sins, past, present, and future, and He was resurrected. God came to be among us, He came to show us the way; if we faith in Him, we, too, will be born again. Resurrected.

Then Jesus said to His deciples, If any man will come after me, let him deny himself, and take up his cross, and follow me. For whosoever will save his life will lose it: and whosoever will lose his life for my sake will find it. (Mathew 16:24-26 KJV)

TREE OF LIFE

THE OLD AND THE NEW

God, made a new covenant with us, and it is the New Testament. Think of it as His will and our inheritance.

Some people are of the opinion that the Old Testament is not important anymore as that was then and this is now. They only want to read the New Testament. I've also heard it said that the Old Testament is the most important as everything we need to know about how to live our lives can be found there.

I've learned that both are equally important. The Old Testament holds the keys to understanding the New Testament. It is intriguing to me that the old prophesizes the new. So much of what is contained in the Old Testament symbolizes Christ by way of shadows and types and heralds the coming of the Messiah. God had a plan from the beginning.

The story of Noah and the ark symbolizes the coming of Christ. Noah can be looked at as a Christophany—a Christlike savior of his time. The ark—a big boat, a temporary dwelling where Noah and his family lived so they would survive the flood.

Moses was another Christophany.

"Thus sayeth the Lord God of the Hebrews, let my people go, that they may serve me" (Exodus 9:1 KJV). God appointed Moses to free His people from captivity.

After leaving Egypt, they wandered in the desert for forty years. During that time, they built a temporary tabernacle everywhere they went to house the Ark of the Covenant-the place where God would dwell among His people.

The specific architecture of the tabernacle, including every piece of furniture housed inside and the materials used to cover the outside, symbolized different aspects of Christ. The placement of each of the tribes around the tabernacle, which was always centered in the camp, had meaning. This is explained in the Old Testament.

In the New Testament, Jesus's body was a tabernacle—a temporary building to dwell among His people. Just take a little time to sit with that. Who is Jesus?

If you want to understand the specifics of the tabernacle of the Old Testament, right down to the measurements involved in the architecture, I challenge you to do your own research to discover the truth. If you need help, then find someone who will teach you. Not someone who teaches you how to live your life based on prevailing trends and opinions, but one who teaches directly from the Bible, chapter by chapter and verse by verse.

Basically, what I'm saying is that you need both the Old Testament and the New Testament. One without the other leads to a lack of understanding of the full message.

Just saying. You can do your own research. Read the Bible, and I promise it will be the best book you will ever read. It can be mind-bending, intriguing, and miraculous. It can be an action-packed thriller, a heartfelt romance, a science fiction, and more. Each story or book within the Bible encompasses so many layers of meaning, and read in its entirety, it will surely dawn on you that it is the greatest story ever told.

I'll admit that I don't have it all figured out yet; I know that I don't have all the answers, but I do know that I will spend the rest of my life reading and studying this book. To my astonishment, every single chapter and verse can be read as they are written and understood on one level. There is the historical account, in the beginning God created the heaven and the earth, the story of Adam and Eve, Noahs Ark, Abraham, Moses and so on. In each story you learn what is pleasing to God and what is depicted as evil. The Ten Commandments given to Moses after the exodus from Egypt listed rules regarding how the people were expected to live righteous lives.

In the New Testament Jesus taught in parables to the masses and he taught the same lessons differently to his desciples. We understand a descipile refers to a follower of Jesus, one of his twelve Apostles. A descipile is a learner, a follower of any particular teacher. An apostle is a messenger, a person who shares the lessons learned with others.

Delve just a bit deeper, dig for the meaning in the original languages and your eyes begin to see, your ears begin to hear, and you may find you have a very different understanding. Forinstance, in English you will read the words, be of good cheer, in many places. Does this mean be happy or joyful? It could be confusing but if you understood the original meaning was to have courage, it can change the context of the story.

I also think there are some mysteries in life we may never fully understand but don't let it be because you didn't even try.

Have you read the Bible? There is a reason that it's the best-selling book of all time and has been translated into more languages than any other book ever published.

There are many great self-help books you can read. I have a fairly sizable library myself. I love all my books. I've learned so much about life, about myself, and each one has little gems of knowledge, something that speaks a bit of truth, something that strikes a chord in my soul.

When a good book speaks to your heart, it's like a new outfit. You try it on, and if it fits right, you wear it for a season until you find a new one. We all grow in our knowledge, piece by piece, or book by book, if you will. I never want to stop learning from others who have experience, knowledge, and wisdom to share.

The Bible is different. It is, in my opinion, the best self-help book ever written. I don't understand it all, and I'll admit I haven't read every single chapter yet. I need help to get through most of it, but just scratching the surface, beginning to understand, I can't get enough.

Just sharing ...

> If God did not exist, it would be necessary to invent him. (Voltaire)

What a thought! Who else could we blame for all our problems or losses, and who would we thank for our successes? I mean think about it: If God didn't exist, we would truly have to take responsibility for our own mystery without any hope of ever knowing anything as truth. How desperately lonely and burdensome would that be?

Would we experience our higher self, have intuition, or know we have a soul? Would we even be aware of something bigger or better, or experience life with any expectation or possibility? Who would we talk to about our deepest darkest thoughts or fears? OMG!

Oh, that too. *Oh my God.* We couldn't use that phrase.

Ha ha! Just thinking.

AND WHAT OF DREAMS

The dreams I dream hold the key to life's little realities. I read the symbols like a novel, looking for that all-important clue that will solve the mystery of my life, take me through my adventure unscathed, and lead me up the right path to follow my purpose.

I dream the dream and then I know the inner weavings of my soul.

This Is What I Know about You

No matter where you are in your life or what your circumstances are, in Gods' heart and mind, you are loved. You are valuable beyond all measure. You are important and unlimited. You absolutely do create your world because you always have a choice. It's never too late. You have a great destiny.

Because you have the gift of free will you always have a choice and the choices you make create your world. Surrender is not about giving up or giving in but it is a state of being humble, being grateful and acknowledging God. With God all things are possible. You are valuable beyond all measure.

DREAMS

The Oracle of S.E.L.F.

Down through the ages, many men and women have recognized the potential within their dreams. Some of them have recorded their thoughts and feelings on the subject, sharing the truths they believed and the wonder they felt when reflection brought inspiration.

> A dream that has not been interpretated is like a letter that has not been opened. (Talmud)

> The tiniest observation may be a window to eternal truth. (Auldous Huxley)

> The human soul is quite a unique entity and the center of all it's secrets is the dream. (Friedrich Hebbel)

> If a man wants his dreams to come true ... he must wake up. (Deepak Chopra)

> Dreams represent the hieroglyphic, the primordial way of expression and the natural speech of the soul. (Charles Baudelaire)

Dr. Sigmund Freud, who was touted as being the

father of dream theory, saw dreams as brimming with symbols. He interpreted most dreams as having sexual overtones and meanings but eventually wrote that this theory could be taken too far. Dr. Carl Jung, who also studied dreams and was a contemporary of Dr. Freud, believed that dreams were actually direct expressions of the mind.

> To dream means to relive one's past, to forget one's present and to get an inkling of one's future. (Wilhelm Stekel)

It's said that dreams are nothing more than electrical impulses in our brain that happen as we sleep and yet I know the process of dreaming is much more than that. We can choose to ignore our dreams or we can use them to help us make sense of our lives. Some of the best ideas are ignited by dreams. They could hold the answer to a quandary that becomes a vaccine, spark the beginning of a great novel or a movie that delights the audience with joy, impart enlightenment or scare the living daylights out of you. It might well be a courageous endeavor to indulge yourself in the possibility that your dreams are an untapped resource of information, or even an unopened gift.

DREAMOLOGY 101

Dreams are, in a sense, biofeedback. Repressed emotions are the basis of illness and the basis of the kind of stress that can impair our immune system. Learn to interpret your dreams. There's a basic formula to understanding the symbology in your dreams. Making use of this wisdom is quite sound, fairly easy to achieve, and within reach of everyone.

Did you know that Jonas Salk received information about the polio vaccine in a dream?

We can use various forms of biofeedback to chart and study different biological functions. During sleep therapy, science can chart the number of times your body changes consciousness, your REM sleep cycle, and even the type of dream you might be experiencing based on EEG (electroencephalogram) testing, which records brain waves; EKG (electrocardiogram) testing, which records the functioning of the heart; and even GSR (galvanic skin response), which can detect the amount of moisture in your pores. All of which come under the heading of biofeedback. Of course, technology has improved over the years, but these are the basic forms of biofeedback, which, independent of each other or combined, can present a more complete picture of the body's response to stimuli or the progression of disease.

In order to raise your arm, you think about performing the action. When you think, your brain creates chemistry, which, in effect, tells your arm to move. Granted, this is a simplistic explanation as I'm not writing a scientific paper.

The pendulum is also a form of biofeedback. Historically, its use has been referred to as an old wives' tale and of no real value. Women used it to tell the sex of unborn babies. It was used by practitioners of the occult to illicit answers to important questions. The pendulum can be as unsophisticated as a safety pin dangling from a string approximately eight to ten inches long or something more elaborate, like a crystal on a chain.

Holding the pendulum in your hand, elbow securely positioned on a table, dangle it over a chart or a map or even a mother's stomach, and ask a question, making sure to not purposely move your arm to keep the pendulum as still as possible. It works because your body has what is called an ideomotor response; in other words, you can't hold your arm or hand completely still as the body reacts to questions or stimuli posed by triggering muscles to move.

It's thought that when asking a question with the conscious expectation of receiving an answer, the subconscious engages the muscles in your arm to move ever so slightly, undetectable, in one direction or another, providing the answer—yes or no, good or bad, boy or girl.

Actually, your body is never completely still, as your heart beats and your lungs expand and contract. If you are completely still, you're probably dead. People continue to use the pendulum, and you can find some beautiful examples in various book stores. Some healers are known to use a pendulum to detect where the body is out of balance, thus enabling them to direct healing energy to that specific area.

Using a handheld GSR monitor, you can learn to relax the body. Working with it on a regular basis helps reduce stress and can assist in lowering your blood pressure. They were all the rage a few decades ago, and you could purchase one from a variety of magazines or shops. I bought mine at RadioShack way back when.

I find it's quite intriguing to use the GSR monitor in conjunction with dream therapy. It takes the client less time to decipher the meaning of the symbols in their dream, thus attaining a more complete picture; less guess work, if you will. You need to work with a therapist who specializes in dream therapy using biofeedback.

Using your dreams as biofeedback is the quickest way to guide you through the steps of discovering what your subconscious believes to be the safest, most productive solution that will benefit the greatest number of people involved. Learn to use your dreams to find creative solutions. Some of the greatest wisdom in the world could be right at your fingertips.

Working with your dreams by using a few simple rules might just open the door to discovering the mystery of you. Why not explore what is bound to be the greatest adventure of your life?

Who am I? Why am I here? What is my purpose? How can I_____? When will I_____? Take the plunge. Immerse yourself in your*self*.

HOW TO USE THE PENDULUM

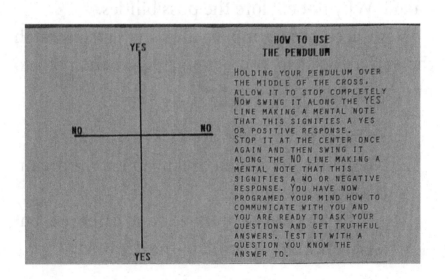

S.E.L.F.—SPIRITUAL, EMOTIONAL LIFE FORCE

Learn to use your dreams to communicate in a very personal way. Dreams are more intimate than being naked. Why not explore the possibilities.

Here are three simple rules that just scratch the surface to help you get started on the path to understanding your dreams.

1. Every detail in your dream is a symbol.
2. No matter whom you dream about, the dream is always about you.
3. All dreams can be prophetic and cathartic, but all dreams are specific to the dreamer.

For instance, if you dream about your mother, the appearance of your mother in the dream is a symbol of what she represents to you. It's what and how you *feel* about your mother. It may bring up emotions of love and memories of apple pie, a perfect example of caring and protection. However, should I dream about my mother, it could symbolize the nightmare of my childhood, as my mother was not very warm or loving. It's the vision of your mother, or even the very word mother, in your dream that triggers a specific emotion or feeling that becomes the clue to what the dream is about.

So a dream is literally a picture diary, which might encompass the past, present, or future. The pictures, or symbols, are like hieroglyphs, and they're connected to specific emotions and feelings. The pictures represent a feeling or even a deeper understanding of an event that you may be currently involved.

Where is your mother in the dream? What is she doing? Are you also in the dream, or are you an observer watching events taking place as if in a movie?

Consequently, there are a few universal ideas, or symbols, that might be logically applied to your dreams. They seem to have like meanings to most people, such as dreaming you are in a car. Conjecture suggests the car symbolizes something to do with the body, the vehicle of your soul. Delve a little deeper; the first question to ask is whether you're the driver or passenger.

If you're driving the car, it could mean that you are in control of where the car is headed, thus in charge of what is happening in your life. If, on the other hand, you find yourself in the passenger seat, it might suggest that you're just along for the ride, which might be delightful in some circumstances, a wonderful adventure, or it could mean that you are not at all in charge of your life, and this may prove disconcerting, to say the least.

Where you see yourself presently, in your dreams, could possibly predict your future or give you a wake-up call. It may be time for you to take hold of the wheel, take control of what is happening in your life, and drive yourself in the direction you truly desire to go.

Fear not. This is just a snapshot of one moment in time.

Change is constant, and knowledge is growth.

Where will I go, what will I do? Oh, fidelty-dee, I'll think about that tomorrow, after all, tomorrow is another day. (Margaret Mitchell)

Truer words were never spoken. There are times when everything just becomes overwhelming and you can't see the forest for the trees. Have you ever been told to "relax, just sleep on it. You'll see, tomorrow in the light of day, everything will seem different"?

Have you ever had a situation where things seemed to be so overwhelming, so out of your control in the moment, you go to sleep that night, wake up the next morning, and either the situation seems to have resolved itself or you realize you have the answer? A thought comes into your head and presents itself as something so simple that you wonder why you didn't think of it yesterday. You have to, at times, surrender, give up or give in to the situation at hand and simply trust.

Just sleep on it.

There are several types of dreams: Message dreams, symbolic dreams, lucid dreams, and prophetic dreams.

My own theory is that dreams are symbolic, prophetic, and specific to the dreamer and all dreams are cathartic, whether you remember them or not. What I am saying is that your dreams are another form of communication. This type of communication is not between two people but between you and your subconscious mind or your soul or even God.

Dreams can illicit visual images, auditory information, nightmares, or even a revelatory message.

> Dreaming about other people is only a symbol—all dreams are about the self. (Loenburg)

In the case of lucid dreams, the dreamer is aware of the fact that they are dreaming, but they continue in the dream. It's been reported that when working with your dreams, you might be able to control what happens. You can literally change the direction of the dream. In fact, you can learn to lucid dream. I find the study of ones' dreams to be fascinating and illuminating.

Have you ever had a dream and, for a minute or two when you first wake up, you are sure that the events really happened? You didn't know you were dreaming, and the events taking place seemed so real. You could literally hear the music, smell the campfire, taste an unusual dish, or feel the touch of a loved one.

I've heard it said that God speaks to us in our dreams.

> In a dream, in a vission of the night, when deep sleep falleth upon men, in slumberings upon the bed. (Job 33:15 KJV)

Then He openeth the ears of men, and sealeth
their instruction. (Job 33:16 KJV)

There are so many instances in the Bible where dreams are mentioned. Dreams show us aspects of our personality, our current state of mind, or help us deal with changes that have occurred in our lives. They can also show us possibilities for the future. The Bible encourages us to pursue our dreams.

If you're interested in pursuing S.E.L.F., there are many books available to help you understand and research specific possibilities and opinions regarding interpretations. Just remember the most important rule is that *you* are *one of a kind* (humankind). We are the many individual facets of a wondrous diamond.

Thank God!

Of course, some of this information is old news, and some of it is downright ancient, but I hope you get the point that dreams are the stuff life is made of. Dreams are a very important and integral to our physical make up. They reflect who and what we are—our*self.*

One mind is in you, is your mind, as there is
only one mind. (Joseph Benner)

The Dreamer's Game

The game's afoot, I've heard it said,
A prize was left upon your bed.
A book explains what must be done;
It's free to play and lots of fun.
Your prize presents a clue for you;
Decipher this, which leads to two.
Decipher them; you're half way there,
Use your wits, don't wait to share.
The game's afoot, I understand.
Again, I say, the dream demands
You play the game with full aband ...
Because the answer's there.

Awake, I dream the daydream;
asleep, I dream the truth.

Dreams are a predominant theme in many different books of the Bible. I prefer to study the King James Version, which is actually the work of approximately fifty different scholars appointed by King James and took twenty-two years to complete. It was dedicated to him.

Although many translations exist, the Bible continues to be reworded, deciphered, and reinterpreted, and it continues to be the best-selling book of all time.

> Come now therefore, and let us slay him, and cast him into some pit, and we will say, some evil beast hath devoured him: and we shall see what will become of his dreams. (Genesis 37:20 KJV)

This is in reference to the story of Joseph, son of Jacob. Some of you may have heard of the story of Joseph and his coat of many colors. Jacob had many sons but Joseph was his favorite and his brothers were jealous of him. Joseph was gifted with the ability to interpret dreams. His brothers sold him into slavery and he was imprisoned. Because he was able to interpret other people's dreams, Pharaoh had him interpret one of his dreams. His gift freed him from prison and he became second in command only to Pharaoh Of course the story is much more involved than my short synopsis and I recommend you take the time to read the whole story.

> As for these four children, God gave them knowledge and skill in all learning and wisdom: and Daniel had understanding in all visions and dreams. (Daniel 1:17 KJV)

> In Gibeon the Lord appeared to Solomon in a dream by night: and God said, ask what I shall give thee. (Kings 3:5 KJV)

> And He said, hear now my words: if there be a prophet among you, I, the Lord will make myself known unto him in a vision, and I will speak to him in a dream. (Numbers 12:6 KJV)

> And it shall come to pass afterward, that I will pour out my Spirit upon all flesh; and your sons and your daughters shall prophesy, your

old men shall dream dreams, your young men shall see visions. (Joel 2:18 KJV)

Proverbs 20:4–5, Jeremiah 29:8–9, Samuel 28:15, Genesis 41:12, Job 33:15–16, Judges 13:13–15, and Numbers 12:6–8 also discuss dreams.

On and on it goes. God speaks to us in our dreams and about our dreams. I invite you to investigate for yourself. Is life the stuff dreams are made of, or are dreams the stuff life is made of? Ever since I was a little girl, I dreamed of writing books and stories.

Merrilee, marrilee, merrilee, merrilee, Life is but a dream. (Eliphalet Oram Lyte)

For there is only one place in all the universe that has been made especially for you, and that is inside your own body. (Hildegard of Bingen)

Suggested Reading:

An Introduction to Dream Interpretation by Manly P. Hall

The Element Encyclopedia of 20,000 Dreams: The Ultimate A-Z to Interpret the Secrets of Your Dreams by Theresa Cheung

The New Secret Language of Dreams: A Visual Key to Dreams and Their Meanings by David Fontana

SOUL THERAPY, A GAME OF INTUITION

The term "soul therapy" is a perfect segue into actually engaging your intuition to interpret your dreams. It's also the title of my first book. You'll forgive me for taking advantage of this synchronistic opportunity to tout my first sharing endeavor.

The whole concept was downloaded into my mind in what seemed like just a few seconds as I was meditating. At the time, I had no intentions other than to open my mind to whatever information might be pertinent for me to know. What a gift.

Soul Therapy incorporates a theory of self-discovery. It's a game that uses twelve cards and implies that intuition, which is inherent for everyone on the planet, can be enhanced by using the concepts presented and focusing on your feelings.

Simply stated, by practicing or working with your intuition, you will definitely create a stronger connection to your higher self—that part of you that is connected to everyone and everything; that part of you that is spontaneously instinctive, sensitive, perceptive, and insightful; and that part of you that is connected to your soul, your awareness of all things spiritual, your frame of mind, your courage, and your character.

We are infinitely different from each other, individual particles of something bigger than ourselves. Whether you choose to call that something bigger the universe or God or something else, we are all connected. Our intuition is innate, an essential characteristic inherited at birth and which evolves with our life experiences. You might say it's part of the toolbox that comes with the soul, like instinct, which triggers our fight-or-flight response.

Soul Therapy is actually much more than a game and those who get it will recognize that it is a catalyst to self-discovery. The link that already exists between your conscious self and your unconscious S.E.L.F.— your spiritual, emotional life force—is something most of us are aware of. This is not supernatural, but it is super and natural.

Playing the game exercises your intuition; like any muscle in the body, it only needs a consistent workout to become stronger. The game is very simple, and the cards depict nothing more than a splash of color. It's how you feel about the color that makes it interesting. You can play the game three different ways. What are you capable of?

Now, I realize that not everyone is interested in playing games or even interested in learning about their own intuition, and that's OK, but if you are the slightest bit curious about understanding the possibilities that exist within yourself or what you might be capable of, then I challenge you to play my little game. You can purchase your own copy of *Soul Therapy* through Balboa Press and on Amazon.

> Expect your intuition to work. When you listen to your inner voice, you become aware of subtle influences. (Sonia Choquette)

> Hundreds of years ago a Sufi Master stated that the value of a book is in what it does—not what is says. (Eldon Taylor)

> The beauty of being intuitive is moving closer to the wisdom of our own hearts. (Judeth Orloff)

> Your life expresses one thing, and one thing only, your state of consciousness. (Neville Goddard)

THOUGHTS ABOUT
PURPOSE

First of all, everyone and everything has purpose. Each and every one of us is intrinsically unique, individual beings of light as numerous as grains of sand or the stars in the universe. In all of time there will never be another you, and you are valuable beyond measure.

I think part of our purpose is to seek, to ask those questions that include why, to look within to connect with something bigger than ourselves, and to discover that as different from each other as we are, we all belong to the universe, or God. At the very least, we belong to the human race. Biologically speaking, it's a miracle that anyone of us is here.

God created us in their own image; after a time, we forgot who *I am*.

And, no, that is not a typo; God, Jesus, and the Holy Spirit are one and the same, different aspects of the One.

God said, "Let US make man in OUR image, after OUR likeness: and let them have dominion over the fish of the sea, and over the fowl of the air, and over the cattle, and over all the earth, and over every creeping thing that creepeth upon the earth" (Genesis 1:26 KJV).

Purpose. Sometimes we confuse our job with our purpose but think of it this way: our job might just be the vehicle by which we choose to pursue our purpose. Our job is what we do and our purpose is more about who we are.

The purpose of life is to live our lives, pursue what brings us joy, and take responsibility for the life we live.

Dear God, if I am chosen, could it be such that seems so small a task as living? I'm sure I'm special, aren't I? It's the reason I'm here, isn't it?

I just know I should be doing something great, something bodacious and wonderful. I should cure cancer or solve climate change. I should be doing something that says, "I'm here; I have arrived!"

I just can't seem to find my purpose in the grand scheme of things. I like my job, most of the time, but that really just pays the rent and puts food on the table. Sometimes I feel so lonely, even in a crowd, even when that crowd is a bunch of my friends. Lord, didn't you create me to be somebody?

This speaks to the yearning to know or understand that we have purpose in the world. We believe that purpose gives us dignity, grace, love, approval, and acceptance. Otherwise, I am nothing but a random spark that never ignited the light within me, so how is it possible to be a light unto or in the world? How can I be a mirror that reflects the light of truth and love if I can't see my own reflection? I think this also encompasses our self-esteem.

Who am I? What am I? What do I have that I can give back to the world? Only myself.

I am what I am. I'm grateful for my life. I love life. I love that I can be the watcher on the wall. I am aware because I can ask the questions and find the answers within. I can only know myself, in everyone, in everything. In that knowing, I live. I am alive. *I am.*

Yes, it's true, God created you and me to be somebody. We start with our first teachers and then we never stop learning, but somewhere down the road, we all become teachers. We teach what we know, and we teach who we are. We teach all the time, whether we are aware that we are teaching or not.

When we smile at a stranger on the street, we teach recognition, acceptance, and love. When we help someone, we teach compassion. When we laugh, we teach joy. When we cry, we teach pain.

We teach who we are and what we are all the time. When we hate, we teach about the hurt and pain in our own lives.

This is why we're here. We are what we teach, and what we teach is who we are. Our purpose is to live our lives with abandon, to find what brings us joy, and then to share it. Either share it with a smile, a tear, a helping hand, or a prayer. How you live your life is your greatest prayer. The purpose of life is to live.

> Prayer is the master key. A key may fit one door of a house, but when it fits all doors it may well claim to be a master key. Such and no less a key is prayer to all earthly problems. (Neville Goddard)

> Mastery of self-control of your thoughts and feelings—is your highest achievement. However, until perfect self-control is attained so that inspite of appearances you feel all that you want to feel, use sleep and prayer to aid you in realizing your desired states. (Neville Goddard)

> Sensation presedes manifestation and is the foundation upon which all manifestation rests. Be careful of your moods and feelings, for there is an unbroken connection between

your feelings and your visable world. (Neville Goddard)

We are so accustomed to wearing a mask, to disguising ourselves to others that we've successfully ended up disguised to ourselves. Our deepest fear is not that we are inadequate. Our deepest fear is that we are powerful beyond our own understanding. It is our light and not our darkness that frightens us because we have no idea what we are truly capable of. We ask ourselves, "Who am I to be brilliant, fabulously happy, talented, gorgeous, and creative?" The real question is, "Who are you not to be?"

Truly, the purpose of life is to seek, to learn, and to find out whom we are from within, and to understand that truth, we must then choose what to do with that knowledge.

Think your mind,
Feel your heart,
Know everything.

We are the ones we have been waiting for.
Look within!

FAVORITE PRAYERS

I love the twenty-third psalm, and if you really want to have a definitive explanation of this well-known prayer, read *The Secret of the Twenty-Third Psalm* by Joel S. Goldsmith. His tiny little booklet will leave you with an immense epiphany concerning the prayer that so many people recite by heart without having a deeper understanding of its meaning.

> God is closer than breathing and nearer than hands and feet. (Alfred Lord Tennison)

> The heading over the Twenty Third Psalm is David's confidence in God's Grace. (Joel S. Goldsmith)

Likewise, the prayer known as the Our Father, which is actually the disciples' prayer as Jesus taught it first to His disciples before He taught it to the multitudes in His Sermon on the Mount (Mathew 6:5 and Luke 11:2–4) I also know by heart.

However, my favorite prayer is the ninety-first psalm. The caption above this psalm reads, "Abiding in God's Care." It always strikes me as odd that when I mention this psalm in conversation, a look of puzzlement comes across the other person's face, and they ask, "Which one is that? I don't know that one."

So I want to take the time to share this prayer and to tell you why it is my favorite.

> [1] He that dwelleth in the secret place of the most High shall abide under the shadow of the Almighty.

> [2] I will say of the Lord, He is my refuge and my fortress: my God, in Him shall I trust.

> [3] Surely he shall deliver thee from the snare of the fowler, and from the noisome pestilence. He shall cover thee with his feathers, and under his wings shalt thou trust. His truth shall be thy shield and buckler. Thou shalt not be afraid of the terror by night, nor for the arrow that flieth by day. Nor from the pestilence that walketh in darkness, nor for the destruction that wasteth at noonday. A thousand shall fall at thy side, and ten thousand at thy right hand; but it shall not come nigh thee. Only with thine eyes shalt thou behold and see the reward of the wicked. Because thou hast made the Lord, which is my refuge, even the most High, thy habitation, there shall no evil befall thee, neither shall any plague come nigh thy

dwelling. For he shall give his angels charge over thee, to keep thee in all thy ways. They shall bear the up in their hands, lest thou dash thy foot upon a stone. Thou shalt tread upon the lion and adder: the young lion and the dragon shall thou trample under feet.

[4] Because he hath set his love upon me, therefore I will deliver him: I will set him on high, because he hath known my name. He shall call upon me, and I will answer him: I will be with him in trouble; I will deliver him and honor him. With long life will I satisfy him, and show him my salvation. (Psalm 91 KJV)

Notice the way I broke the psalm up into four paragraphs, because this prayer is actually a three-way conversation between the angel of the Lord (a messenger, if you will), the person reciting the prayer, and God.

In the first paragraph, the angel tells the person reciting the prayer that if they dwell on the Lord in that secret place of the Most High, He will listen to them and respond.

The second paragraph is a declaration by the person reciting the prayer. "I will say of the Lord, he is my refuge and my fortress: my God, in him will I trust." That's it; the person's only part in this prayer. A declaration of faith. The only thing one has to do is have faith.

The third paragraph is the angel speaking again, telling the person reciting the prayer all that God will do for them and that no matter what the turmoil or the circumstances the supplicant might be experiencing, God will even send his angels to hold them up, to protect them.

The last paragraph is spoken by God, who joins the conversation and, indeed, states that He will recognize the supplicant. God further states that because of the person's faith and trust in Him and love for Him, He will be there for them, deliver them, and show them salvation.

When you say this prayer, you will have a much deeper understanding if you can comprehend the conversation taking place. I've heard it said that the ninety-first psalm is truly one of the most powerful prayers you can say.

I read this prayer when I was younger, when I was troubled. I really had no idea what I was saying. I just knew I was desperate and I needed help. I needed God to intercede on my behalf, and I fully trusted that He would help me with what I was going through at the time. Later when I learned that this was a three-way conversation, it definitely made a difference for me; my declaration is evermore fervent.

The most important thing that I can tell you is that God has come to my rescue, over and over. I always ask for help using this prayer and He has always answered my plea.

THE NINTY-FIRST PSALM

REINCARNATION
VERSUS RESURECTION

As promised, we will now contemplate this idea further. The first point of distinction came for me when I was interested in Buddhism and seeking to understand more about reincarnation.

I love the Dalai Lama and his peaceful, joyful demeanor, and I've read several of his books. I refer to Tenzin Gyatso, the fourteenth Dalai Lama and recipient of the Nobel Peace Prize in 1989.

Delighted to have the opportunity to see the Dalai Lama in person at a conference in Long Beach, California, my expectations were high. I fully expected to be enlightened by what he had to say. I will tell you that I was not disappointed. While I won't bore you with my naivety nor my romantic ideas about becoming a Buddhist, I will tell you that I was indeed enlightened that day on many levels.

During a question-and-answer segment, an older woman in the crowd asked, "Is it possible for someone like me to become a Buddhist?" At this point I was all ears.

After an endearing little chuckle, he answered her with another question. "Do you believe in God?"

The woman answered rather robustly, "Yes!"

The Dali Lama then continued, "No. You can't be a Buddhist if you believe in God."

Needless to say, I was in shock. How did I miss this? Buddhism does not recognize a creator god. Just to be fair, as it turns out, this doesn't mean that all Buddhists are atheists or agnostics. Furthermore, everyone is entitled to believe what they choose for themselves, and I'm not making any judgements about what anyone else chooses to believe.

Just sharing …

I walked away more than grateful for the opportunity and, having thoroughly enjoyed the day, I realized that my search would have to continue. Sometimes the dictionary is helpful, but in this case, I still needed a more definitive answer to my question concerning the difference between reincarnation and resurrection.

Back to my little example of the caterpillar and the butterfly.

Simply put, one might say that the caterpillar reincarnated into a butterfly. Indeed, it becomes, or reincarnates, into another body to live a different life. Instead of a creeping insect on the ground, it flies, but it is still a bug. (Hint: we are not bugs.)

My way of thinking is that the butterfly might be a perfect example of reincarnation. I'm sure there must be other examples in nature that demonstrate and perpetuate this idea as well.

We were created to have dominion over all the animals, every fish in the sea and every creeping life-form. We are something different. What I understood, *at that time*, was that Christ died and no longer being in that physical body, resurrected into something else, a different type of body. It seemed logical to me that reincarnation and resurrection might be synonymous. No one I knew could answer my question, or they didn't really want to have this conversation. Still, I knew I needed to know. Something still nagged at me. There was more to this that I needed to understand. I just didn't have a sufficient answer.

The dictionary is my first go-to book for explanations. Haha! The jokes on me. Wrong book. I was going to all these other churches and teachers seeking answers. I do believe that all churches serve a purpose and basically teach the same premise— love your neighbor, do no harm, be of service to your fellow man, yada, yada, yada. What I wasn't doing was reading or studying the Bible. I had no idea that this is where I could find all my answers.

I have to add that another missing piece would be finding the right teacher who can help you navigate and understand what you're reading. The King James Version resonated with me, and I also found the right teachers (plural) who could explain things with the help of the original text (i.e., translate Hebrew, Aramaic, and Greek.)

Our English translators for the most part performed their duties admirably but occasionally resorted to creative translations for certain repetitive words. For instance, in English, you might read the words, "Be of good cheer or have cheer," when the original text in Greek reads, "have courage." This changes the concept of what you're reading considerably.

Going back to the beginning, I now know the difference between reincarnation and resurrection definitively, without a doubt in my mind or my heart or my soul.

Maybe you already know this, or maybe you're not sure. Wherever you are in your search, beliefs, or understanding, the answer to this is all right there in the very beginning of the book of Genesis. As I said, the Old Testament is vital to understanding the New Testament.

God is my Creator, and as such, I was with Him before I was born in this earthly body, or better said, this clay tabernacle. It's a temporary house for my soul that grants free will in order for me to understand my purpose and make a choice. When I die and shed this tabernacle, my soul will return to God in Heaven. (I am who I am.)

Short and simple. Maybe a little too simple, for surely there's a lot more to the story, which is what Jesus came to teach us. As you might suspect, I still have a lot of questions about many other things, and I will continue my studies, but regarding this specific topic, I am clear.

So what *is* reincarnation? Here's what I think. Reincarnation is a good theory that might explain why some people seemingly have memories of another life lived in another time in history. Possibly those memories reside in our DNA.

If you could contemplate for just a moment that these memories might be incorporated in our DNA, and as preposterous as this might sound, it could make sense when you consider that everything we are is recorded in our DNA. The color of our eyes, what we look like, our ethnic heritage, even what diseases we might be prone to experience at some point in our lives - though some of those diseases are understood to skip a generation - everything we are is inherited from our family. We inherit things from our mothers and our fathers, from our grandparents and so on and so on as far back as you can track.

For instance, I have a rare congenital condition that is normally passed down from mother to daughter. When I signed up for 23andMe my DNA showed that indeed, my mother passed it down to me and she got it from her mother and so on as far back as I could tract the women in my family, it was there. Another interesting tidbit of information I discovered was that apparently an unusually high amount of Neanderthal showed up in my DNA. For some people, having their DNA tested can be surprising, and even fascinating.

Of course, I don't have memories that lead me to believe that at one time I actually lived the life of a Neanderthal. However, years before I had my DNA tested, I did believe that I could remember an earlier lifetime in England and when I actually visited England, I experienced feelings of de' ja' vu and felt at home, like I belonged. After I tested my DNA, I discovered that my heritage is English, Irish and Scottish; *aha*. That just made perfect sense. This was interesting for me because I was adopted and pretty much clueless about my heritage.

Just like dreams, which some people are able to remember in great detail, and still others are able to easily decipher the symbology, looking for specific messages, the memory of what is perceived as having lived another lifetime could be a different kind of memory or message for that individual.

Although, for those people who are capable of remembering living another life in such great, uncanny detail, I believe more research is needed on this subject in conjunction with DNA.

I am quite confident that this would be very different from dreams, which occur during sleep and can simply be cathartic but common and necessary for the well-being of the individual. There must be a purpose in believing you remember living another life.

Feeling or believing you have lived another life, if indeed, you are experiencing what I propose could be DNA memory, is far less prevalent an experience, although a very popular muse and seemingly lends credence to the idea of reincarnation.

Still, there must be purpose in this type of memory, as God doesn't do anything without purpose. So there must be a reason behind this specific experience.

There would be, in my estimation, some kind of information or a lesson of a different kind than that of dreams.

> Serenity is not freedom from the storm, but
> peace amidst the storm. (Jefferson Wright)

Truth

One truth is this and then it's that.
Who pulls the rabbit from their hat?
Each of us in our own way
Needs to learn to speak and say
The truth as we all see it best,
But truth is just a place to rest.
Truth is where we walk our path,
But truth will lead us all, at last,
Home to where the words are gone,
For words are merely but a song
That carries us and takes us home,
One and all, not alone.

Blackbird singing in the dead of night, take these broken wings and learn to fly, all your life, you have only waited for this moment to arrive. (The Beatles)

I think virtual reality is a lie. It's all real. Virtual is the lie. Think dimensionally. You may have no real understanding of just how thin the veil between the many dimensions of thought is, thus you may be lulled into trusting that nothing is real.

Reality
Evolves
All
Life

> I would not interfere, with any creed of yours, nor want it to appear, that I have all the cures. There is so much to know, so many things are true, the way my feet must go, may not be best for you. And so I give a spark, of what is light to me, to guide you through the dark, but not tell you what to see. (Unknown)

RESOLUTION A
REVELATION

Therefore speak I to them in parables: because they seeing see not, and hearing they hear not, neither do they understand. (Mathew 13:13 KJV)

Repeatedly, you've read the words knowing is growing. A catchy little phrase that could mean that as you learn, you grow in your understanding of various concepts, that understanding something new or even changing your opinion about something you thought you knew brings about a maturity in your mind and in your soul, which eventually includes your physical self, or how you conduct yourself in the world. Your body, mind, and spirit are changed. One cannot happen without effecting the other. In other words, your spiritual, emotional life force (S.E.L.F.) is changed. Now, this is nothing new.

Knowing is growing is also a double entendre. It could mean that more people than ever before are now in the know, that, in the past, what only a few understood, now is considered to be common knowledge.

Not too long-ago things like meditation, Reiki, yoga, and even the use of crystals in healing were scoffed at by those who didn't understand. However, our views on how we administer to the health and well-being of the human body has radically changed. It would seem that science and spirituality are no longer at odds with each other but, in fact, complement each other.

Science has grown into the knowledge that spirituality is vital to the health and well-being of the body and that spirituality is no longer relegated strictly to religious fervor. Things that were taboo before are now generally accepted as truth.

Our world has changed drastically and at the speed of light. What we understood one hundred years ago, has transformed exponentially over the last fifty years. Keeping up with those changes has also brought with it the evidence of an even greater knowledge of the suffering that is rampant for both those who have understanding and those who still grapple with it.

Analogous to all that rhetoric, I want to change the conversation back to the Bible in the hopes that you might be inspired to open one if you haven't yet. If you don't own or can't afford one, all you have to do is Google "free Bible". The list of resources is abundant. By the way, it isn't important where you start, just as long as you start somewhere. It isn't important which version of the Bible you choose, as there are many, so start with what speaks to you.

I know that the first book in the Old Testament usually causes eyes to roll backward because all that begetting seems daunting and boring. You know what I'm talking about. So-and-so begat so-and-so, who begat so-and-so, and so on. Pretty dry reading, you might think.

For example, Genesis 5 specifically lays out the genealogy of Adam's lineage. I could say it's a record of the "Adams' family," just to get a little chuckle, but it is the record of the family of man.

Recently, I was made aware of something, a little hidden tidbit of information that, for me, was quite interesting. I'm sure you know that every name has meaning, including those names in the Bible, whether in the Old Testament or the New Testament. Nothing in the Bible is without intent or purpose.

Remember that I told you both testaments are intertwined and that one reflects or is interwoven with the other. They both sometimes hold hidden meanings purposely left for us to discover if we choose to see what we're reading and hear with our hearts.

The following list is from Joseph Prince of Joseph Prince Ministries. On the left, you see a list of Adam's lineage (who begat who) as it is recorded in Genesis 5. On the right, you'll see the equivalent meaning of each of those names.

Adam—man
Seth—appointed
Enosh—mortal
Kanen—sorrow
Mahalelel—the blessed God
Jared—will come down
Enoch—teaching
Methusala—his death shall bring
Lamech—powerful
Noah—rest

When you string together the meanings of these names, it's possible you'll find they can otherwise be read in this way:

"Man, appointed, mortal, [is] sorrow, [but] the Blessed God will come down teaching, [and] His death shall bring powerful rest."

My mind lit up after hearing and seeing this for myself, because of course I had to look it up. What an intriguing interpretation. Once again, it was obvious to me how important the Old Testament is to understanding the New Testament. How intricately they are woven together. Some of those names are from the Old Testament and others from the New Testament.

Again, the beginning foretells the ending. Adam and Eve transgressed against God's edicts; therefore, much to their sorrow and ours, they were evicted from the Garden of Eden. But God had plans, because He loved His creation, His children. He didn't want to destroy them. So He planned to teach them. He would dwell among them, maybe many times, before they would understand the lesson, and finally He would physically dwell with them one last time. He would demonstrate the truth of love and the truth about who we are. He would send His Son to sacrifice His life on our behalf. Forgiveness would bring us powerful rest or peace. Like the Prodigal Son, our Father is patiently waiting with open arms to bring us back into the garden.

While I'm not sure exactly what reference materials were used concerning the meanings of those specific names, I was able to simply Google the meanings so it is obviously common knowledge. I found the sentiments behind the meanings beautiful. Something that might require further research or study by you, which is the whole point of this story.

I wanted to share this delightful message as one interpretation in order to point out the fact that all interpretations of what we read in any Bible are wholly individualized and based on what we believe. You believe a specific interpretation not because someone said it is the truth but because it strikes a chord of understanding in your heart and soul as truth and I hope it inspires you to look for more.

Knowing is growing, and we each hold a little bit of the truth about whom we are as a tiny seed imbedded in our hearts. For each of us, the sound of truth rings a bell and that tiny seed begins to grow in understanding within its soul, which is your soul.

We are planted in the soil of our community garden, and some of what has been planted begins to grow out of the dirt. Peeking out of that soil, we stretch and grow, ever facing upward toward the sun for warmth.

The Gardener affectionately tends His field, supplying us with all the water and nutrients needed so we can grow healthy and strong. He waits patiently for us to produce a bud from the seed He planted, and He is delighted when that bud begins to unfold.

Persevering with mercy, the Gardener coddles each and every bud and tends the soil by weeding out what He didn't plant and removing the bugs and other pests that have found us to be tasty morsels.

When the season is right, those of us who have fully bloomed are lovingly gathered together. We adorn the center of His table, and He is gratified in His devotion to the bouquet He has created.

THE GARDEN

Points of Interest:

- Seven lines on the ground. (Seven is the number of completion.)
- Five petals on each of the three blooms. (Five is the number of grace)
- 3 x 5 = 15. When added together, 1 + 5 = 6. (Six is the number of man)
- The spiral in the sun symbolizes eternity.
- The diamond in the sky above the sun represents God.

All things are made by imagination's power. Nothing begins except in the imagination of man. "From within out" is the law of the universe. "As within, so without." Man turns outward in his search for truth, but the essential thing is to look within. (Nevel Goddard)

The surface mind was never intended to be the center of consciousness. Rather, it is an avenue of awareness in much the same manner that the five senses are avenues of awareness. The eyes are the mechanism, but the mind does the seeing. The ears are the mechanism, but the mind does the hearing. The surface mind, in turn, is the mechanism, an avenue of contact with the world for the true center of consciousness deeper in your being. (Ruby Nelson)

There is therefore now no condemnation for them which are in Christ Jesus, who walk not after the flesh but after the spirit. (Romans 8:1 KJV)

And if children, then hiers, heirs of God, and joint heirs with Christ; if so be that we suffer with him, that we may be also glorified together. (Romans 8:17 KJV)

While in human form yet, your expression was so entirely impersonal, that, though self-conscious, you still looked to me within, for inspiration and guidance. (Joseph Benner)

Just as Emmerson wrote his poem about the meaning of a successful life, the following is my own answer to that question.

Understand that being humble means finding gratitude in everything. View love from God's point of view and share that with everyone. Believe in the oracle of S.E.L.F., which is your spiritual, emotional life force, and trust in that. Hear the music of life and sing your song aloud. Know grace. This is a successful life.

If we don't stand for something, we fall for anything. (Pastor Melissa Scott)

Tharseo (Pronounced tar-sai) means "have courage; be of good cheer."

Everything must have meaning
or nothing has meaning.
Thank you for taking the time
to entertain my words.

ABOUT THE AUTHOR

Artist, author, and teacher, Ms. Quintana is a graduate of the Behavioral Science Research and Education Center. She is a Reiki master and teacher and an ordained minister. She taught dream interpretation at Unity Church and was art coordinator for The Ian M. Hassette Foundation. She is the author of *Soul Therapy: A Game of Intuition*, which teaches readers how a simple game can strengthen your intuition. Her first book was nominated for the Eric Hoffer Award. Ms. Quintana has been recognized by Maquis Who's Who in America 2022/2023. She is an award-winning poet and continues to teach art classes offered at Grace Harbor Studio located in her home in California. Her artworks are available for sale in several local galleries and at FineArtAmerica.com.

Printed in the United States
by Baker & Taylor Publisher Services